Contemporary Monologues for Young Actors

DOUGLAS M. PARKER

*For my mother, who told me that anything is possible,
and for my father, who made me believe it.*

TABLE OF CONTENTS

INTRODUCTION

Generally speaking, the monologues in this book were written for actors and acting students aged 7-14, as well as for the teachers, directors and acting coaches who work with them. Some of the monologues may work better for actors toward the lower end of that age range, while others may work better for actors toward the upper end. There is no particular order to the monologues presented, but more of the monologues toward the beginning of the book may work better for slightly younger actors, while more of the later monologues may work better for slightly older actors.

Whether you're a teacher, actor or student – and whether your goal is to instruct, learn, perform or audition – as you browse through this book, simply choose for yourself or your students whatever monologues feel right.

A QUICK WORD FOR ACTORS

These monologues can be used for auditions, as short performance pieces, or simply to sharpen your acting skills. When choosing your monologues, keep in mind that all of the performance pieces in this book were created to work equally well for male actors and female actors. The monologues you choose should simply be a matter of selecting the pieces that move you, amuse you, or that you feel a connection with. Others may present a character or emotion you want to explore.

Once you've chosen a monologue, if it makes you feel more comfortable with the material to change a word or a name, go ahead and do it. Think of the monologues as tools and yourself as the artist. Whatever helps you deliver the best possible performance is what you should be doing.

Similarly, you'll find that some of the monologues have small performance suggestions before the monologue itself, or some minor stage directions within the body of the monologue. Acting is about bringing your own interpretation to the words – so feel free to ignore the stage directions and bring the monologue to life in your own way.

Finally, always take the time to think about what each character in each monologue you perform is really saying and really feeling. As long as you find the heart of the moment, the heart of the character and, most importantly, your own heart, you'll never go far wrong.

SHARING

Some people think I don't like sharing, but that isn't true at all. I love sharing. I mean, what's not to love about being able to go up to someone and say, "Hey, can I have some of that candy?" And then they give you some! Or, "Can I ride your bike for a while?" And then you get to ride their bike! Sharing is awesome. Sometimes you have to be careful, though. Like if someone comes up to me and says, "Can I have one of your cookies?" Well, if I gave them a cookie, then I might not have any cookies left to share with other people and that would be, like, the opposite of sharing. So I have to say no. Because sharing is really important.

BUGS

I like bugs. A lot. Spiders, ants, beetles, scorpions. Most people don't even know that scorpions are insects. They think they're lizards or something. But they're not. Even lobsters are related to spiders. Yeah. So enjoy your dinner. Everyone's always telling me that bugs are disgusting. But I say, if you can like dogs, why can't you like bugs? Truth is, most dogs are covered with bugs anyway. So every time you pet your dog, you're really just petting a bunch of bugs. Even I wouldn't do that. Yeah. Now who's the disgusting one?

WAITING

(Your character is staring at the clock, waiting for the end of the school year.)

The last five minutes before the end of the school year has to be the longest five minutes in the world. Seriously. Entire planets have been formed and exploded in less time. And it doesn't help that this clock is definitely broken. Look at how slow the second hand is moving. Tick . . . . . . .Tock . . . . Tick. Why doesn't somebody fix that thing? Come On! It's not like the janitor has anything better to do. Good grief – I think I just saw the second hand move backwards. Hold on. Was that . . . ? Yes! The minute hand just moved up one minute!

(Stare at the clock for an extended moment.)

Sheesh. The last four minutes before the end of the school year has to be the longest four minutes in the world.

SCOUT

Before we moved here, we had this big dog named Scout. Mom always said he was a total mutt, but I think he was also part collie. And maybe part golden retriever. But he was definitely at least half mutt. Scout was supposed to be the whole family's dog, but he was really mine. I mean, after school, it was me he would be waiting for. And when anyone threw his ball, I'm the one he always brought it back to. And at night, it was always my bed he slept in. But before we moved here, my Mom found out we weren't allowed to have any pets, so we had to give him away to my cousins. I don't really talk about it, but sometimes I dream about Scout. He's got his ball in his mouth and he's looking for me. And I'm saying, "Here, Scout. I'm right here." But he doesn't hear me, and he can't see me, and I'm saying, "I'm right here. Scout. I'm right here." And then, I don't know, I guess I wake up . . . I don't know if Scout dreams about *me*.

GUMMY BEARS

The difference between thinking about having no school all summer and actually having no school all summer is like the difference between thinking about Gummy Bears and actually eating them. I mean, when you think about Gummy Bears and imagine eating them, it's so easy to remember how sweet they are. And how chewy. And that they're really, really good. I mean Gummy Bears are REALLY good. But the truth is, the only thing that imagining eating Gummy Bears does for you is make you even hungrier for Gummy Bears. But on the other hand, imagining not having school all summer . . . I mean, actually not having school all summer . . . I forget what I was gonna say . . . Does anyone have any Gummy Bears?

RIDE

(Your character is riding a roller coaster and not liking it at all. These are the thoughts that are going through your character's mind. NOTE: For this monologue, you should be sitting in a chair. Make sure to use your body to show when the coaster is going up and when it's going down.)

(Going up.)

Omigod, omigod, omigod, omigod. I don't know why I ever got on this thing. I hate roller coasters. I've always hated roller coasters. I should never have listened to what Chris said. Whoa – here come's the top and – AAAAGH!

(Going down fast.)

How is this fun? This is not fun. This is no fun at all. AAAAGH!

(Going up.)

Omigod, omigod, omigod, omigod, we're going up again. And we're going higher. And we're going higher. Why don't they have a stop in the middle of this thing to let people out? That would be a good idea. They should have – AAAAGH!

(Going down fast.)

Just hold on. Just hold on. Just hold on. AAAAGH! WE'RE ALL GONNA DIE!

(Leveling off.)

OK, OK, OK, we're slowing down. We're on the ground. We're slowing down. We're stopping. Yes. Yes. Yes. It's over.

(To a friend in the coaster next to you.)

What? Yeah, really fun. Let's go home.

BROCCOLI

Why does broccoli even exist? For one thing, it's gross. For another thing, it's disgusting. And for a third thing, it's ugly. Well, someone has to say it. Broccoli is ugly. Like, think about French fries. French fries are a vegetable too. But they're not gross . . . unless they're cold. And they're totally not ugly. I mean, hello – they're *golden*. In what universe is gold not a good thing? And did I mention broccoli tastes bad? Yeah, basically broccoli has nothing at all going for it. Except that my Mom likes it. And tries to make me eat it. Did I mention that broccoli is disgusting?

SILENCE

(Your character is reading a book and talking to an unseen person nearby who just won't stop talking. Begin by reading the book silently. After a few moments, without looking up, hold up your hand in a "Stop" gesture towards the unseen person and begin the monologue.)

Stop talking. Just stop talking . . . No . . . Nope . . . Un unh.
(Lower your hand and continue reading for a few moments, then look up at the unseen person.)
I'm sorry, did you say something? . . . That's what I thought. Don't.
(Go back to reading the book for several moments. When you speak again, don't look up.)
You know, I can see your mouth moving. And I can hear sounds coming out of it. That must mean you're talking. Remember that part where I said, *Don't?* Well, don't.
(Reading the book for several more moments. Close the book and look up.)
OK, I'm finished. Hey – where are you going? . . . Well, it's not like I . . . What?!? . . . Fine . . . Gah! Some people are so sensitive.

TRUST

My uncle says there are two kinds of people. People you can trust and people you can't trust. The people you can trust are the ones you *know* are out to get you. The people you can't trust are the ones you don't know if they're out to get you or not. Undependable, I guess.

When I grow up, I want to be just like my uncle. He's super smart. And really, really rich. He's so rich that he always has a bunch of people around him just to do whatever he says. Some of them will even do whatever he says before he says it. And he's got three houses. Three! And he hardly ever lives in any of them. So I know he must be right about the not-trusting-people thing. The only thing is, if he *is* right, how I do I know I can trust what he says?

DIARY

(Your character is writing in a diary.)

Dear Diary. Today was the worst day of my whole life. Everyone was mean to me. At recess, I stepped in a puddle in my brand new sneakers. When I got home, I saw that my goldfish had died. And then my brother stole my allowance. It was so bad that if I could go back and change everything, I'd . . .

(Stop. Think a moment. Start to smile. Now, as you re-read your diary entry out loud, you'll be crossing out the bad things you've just written and writing in good things in their place.)

Dear Diary. Today was the . . .

(Cross out "worst" and write in a new word.)

. . . *best* day of my whole life. Everyone was . . .

(Cross out the old "bad" thing and write in the new good one.)

. . . really, really nice to me, because they like me so much. At recess, I stepped in a puddle . . .

(Cross out the old "bad" thing. Think a moment, then write.)

. . . of diamonds.

(Think another moment, then write again.)

. . . And rubies. In my brand new sneakers. Which everyone said were the best sneakers ever. When I got home, I saw that my goldfish had died . . .

(Write.)

. . . after being abducted by aliens. And then my brother stole my allowance. But he got caught by Mom and Dad, and they told him that they were ashamed of him and that he is the worst brother in the world. And then they sent him to his room and told him not to come out until he is as smart, good-looking, fun and likeable as me . . . The . . . end.

FROG

So every year after summer ends, they make everybody in the whole class get up and talk about what they did all summer. Not all at once. Like one at a time. Booooring. And embarrassing. I don't even know what's worse, having to listen to everyone else's lame summer or having to stand up there in front of everyone else and talk about my own incredibly lame summer. Seriously. I have to stand up there and say things like, "And then one day, my Dad took us all fishing and I caught a frog!" Whatever. (*Pause.*) You want to know about my summer? Fine. Monday, woke up. Went to bed. Tuesday, woke up. Went to bed. Wednesday, woke up, had a fight with my brother, was sent to bed.

But then one day, my Dad really did take us fishing, at this pond over in Maguire Park and this stupid frog somehow wound up getting stuck on my hook. And this . . . this stupid frog, he was like, gasping. Like screaming without any sounds coming out. And his eyes were really wide open, and he was just looking at me, like, I don't know, like "how could you do this?" Or like, "help me." Or, I don't know, like, "all I wanted was a nice day in the park, too." And my little brother was crying. And my Mom was yelling at my Dad to do something. And my Dad said, "It's OK, Jess." And he pulled the frog off the hook and put him on the ground, and I saw the frog, like, hop away a little bit funny, but I think he was OK . . . I'm pretty sure he was OK. And then the next day, I got up, had a fight with my brother, and was sent to bed early.

PROBLEM

I have a drinking problem . . . When I drink, I pee. And that's a problem. The thing is, though, that I love to drink. Orange soda. Grape soda. Ginger ale. Coke. Pepsi . . . Orange juice. Apple juice. I love the juice. Last week, we went on a field trip to, like, an hour away by bus. I knew I shouldn't have drunk two Cokes before we got on the bus, but I did it anyway. Maybe halfway there, I really had to pee. I mean *really* had to pee. And I said to Mrs. McCready, "I really have to pee." She said, "Can you hold it?" And I said, "No. I think I waited too long to tell you. I have to go *now.*" So, in front of the whole class, she says to the bus driver, "We need to pull over. Taylor has to pee." I thought I was gonna die. If I didn't explode first. When I got back on the bus, everyone was laughing. You better believe I only drank *one* Coke on the way back.

SHOPPING

So I was in the clothing store with my Mom and I saw that this girl I kind of know from up the street, named Jenna, actually works there. So I said to my mom, "You know, I can shop for my own clothes. I don't need your help." And she said, "I've seen what you pick out when I'm not around and that's not gonna happen." Arggh! And this girl Jenna is looking over and I know she can hear us and she comes right over and says to my mother, "May I help you?" I wanted to die. And my mom says, "Yes, we're looking for a pair of pants – nothing too tight." Oh, my God! So Jenna brings out this pair of jeans from, like, the 90's or the Roman Empire or something and I have to put them on. And I'm standing in front of the mirror and my mom says to Jenna, "Don't you think they're a little too tight in the . . . you know." And Jenna stares right at my . . . you know . . . and says, "Don't worry, Mrs. Crawley. No one's even gonna be looking there." The next day I told my mom that the dog had chewed the pants up.

ASSIGNMENT

(Your character is presenting a writing assignment to the class.)

Well, as you all know, Mr. Patterson told us we had to write a hundred-word essay about something we did this weekend, so here goes.

My Boring Trip to the Thompson Valley Supermarket, by Alex Grundel.

This weekend, I was sitting around the house having a really good time watching TV when my Mom came in and said I had to go with her to supermarket.

So we drove all the way to Thompson Valley and when we got inside the supermarket, we went right to aisle seven, which is where they keep all the cereal. And I said, "Can we get Fruit Loops?" But my Mom said we couldn't, because they have too much sugar. So I said, "Well, you're the one who's always telling me I need to be sweeter." But she didn't think that was funny, so we got Raisin Bran instead.

Then we got some milk and some chicken and some vegetables and some Hot Pockets. And then she asked me if I wanted anything special and I said, "Yeah, the last twenty minutes of my life back," and so we just paid and went home. Fortunately, I had remembered to record the rest of my TV show before we left, so I got to see the end of it anyway.

BASKETBALL

(Your character is in the middle of a basketball game.)

Morgan! Morgan! I'm open! Dude, I'm open! Throw me the ball! I have a clear shot! . . . Nooo! Don't throw it to Devon. Devon never gets it in . . . OK, so he/she got that one in . . . Alright! . . . Alright, alright – ball's in play! Yeah, show him/her what you've got, Pat! Show him/her what you've got! Grab it! Yeah! Yeah! Yeah! Good job! I'm open! Pat, I'm open! Dude – right here!

(Awkwardly catching the ball, which was unexpectedly thrown right towards your face.)

Whoa! What the . . . ?

(Throwing the ball badly towards the basket and missing.)

Sorry! Sorry! I lost my balance . . . Whoa – good save! Yeah! Morgan! . . . Morgan! . . . Morgan! . . . Morgan! . . . I don't get it. Why doesn't anyone ever throw it to me?

BEAUTIFUL

My mother says that when it comes to people, there are two kinds of beautiful. There are people who are beautiful on the outside, and people who are beautiful on the inside. She says that if you're beautiful on the outside, it's easier for you to get what you need. But if you're beautiful on the inside, it's easy for you to help other people get what *they* need. I guess my mom couldn't decide what kind of beautiful she wanted to be, so she just picked both.

HOME

I have two moms. I also have two dads. And two brothers, and one sister, and I'm also an only child. Well, half the time I'm an only child. That's because my biological parents got divorced practically as soon as I was born. And then before I can even remember, they both got married again to other people. So basically, I've had two sets of parents my entire life. One of my moms is really easy – she'd probably give me anything I asked for. The other one is really tough, but she's the first one to defend me whenever I get in trouble. And the first one to punish me after. And my dads are totally different, too. Like one of them has been the coach of almost every soccer team I've ever been on. The other one couldn't care less about sports, but he taught me the guitar *and* the harmonica. People always ask me if it's confusing having four parents, but it really isn't like that. It's more like, in my life they each found a different place for themselves. And when you put all those places together – well, I guess that's home.

NICE THINGS

I really like nice things and when I see them, I just want to have them. A lot. Maybe too much. Because sometimes nice things, like from stores or school or other people's houses, they just wind up in my pocket. I don't really *mean* to take them, but I just, you know, I *do*. And then the ridiculous thing is, I can't even keep them, because everyone – especially my Dad – would say, "Hey, where did you get that really nice . . . whatever?" And then what would I say? So even the stuff that winds up in my pocket – the really nice stuff that I really, really want – I always just take it back the next day anyway.

SICK

(Your character is describing what it feels like when he or she is about to throw up.)

It happens every winter when I get the flu. It only takes a few seconds, but it's the worst feeling in the world – especially since I know what's coming but there's nothing I can do to stop it. The whole thing always starts really small, with just a little tingling in the tips of my fingers. I almost wouldn't notice it, except that a few seconds later my forehead gets all sweaty. And then I feel like a million ants are crawling all over my body – everywhere. And that's when I know what's coming. All of a sudden my arms and legs feel really cold and my chest feels empty and my mouth fills up with saliva and I just BLURGHHHH! AAACK. Ufff. If I'm lucky, I make it to the bathroom first.

PIANO LESSONS

Last month, I started taking piano lessons with Mrs. Uletsky up the street and already I can tell I'm above average. Like way above average. If I just play a song maybe two or three times, it sounds *perfect*. I mean, not to everybody – and definitely not to Mrs. Uletsky. But without hardly practicing at all, I can make almost any song that only takes one hand sound amazing. Seriously, almost every note is almost exactly right. And the notes that aren't almost exactly right, I can just totally ignore. It's like they never even happened. Mrs. Uletsky says that if don't start applying myself, I'll never get anywhere, but not everyone recognizes talent when they see it.

VOTE

Hi, my name is Terry Taylor and you should vote for me for class president, because of all the really amazing ideas I have to make all of our lives here at Garfield a better place. Like, OK, for instance, this one idea that I have that there should be a table out in the hallway all the time filled with free cookies and cupcakes and brownies and maybe those amazing frittata bites that they sell at Mr. Chocho's down on the corner. I mean, if everyone likes frittata bites or even knows what they are. They're really good. This would improve school morale and also keep everyone's energy up for better studying.

Another amazing idea I have is to completely get rid of grades, mostly because I think they're elitist and also because even someone who fails is actually a successful person in their own way. So there's that.

And finally, I would like to introduce a by-law or something that would make it socially not acceptable for anyone to be called a geek or maybe shoved into a locker or have their lunch money stolen just because they maybe wear glasses or, for instance, are running for class president. So there's that. Thank you . . . Terry Taylor. Vote for Terry Taylor . . . Thank you.

CANDY

(Your character is at the counter at a corner store.)

Two Snicker Bars, please.

(Taking out the money and putting it on the counter.)

Here you go . . . What? . . . *How* much? . . . It was like fifty cents less yesterday . . . Well, I don't have it. Can I pay you tomorrow? . . . Are you kidding me? I'm in here almost every day. I'm probably your best customer. You should be paying *me*! . . . I am NOT raising my voice . . . No, I'm not! NO, I'M NOT! . . . Fine. Keep the Snicker Bars. I don't even like them anyway.

(Walk all the way to the door of the candy store. Just at the door, look back, think a moment or two, then go back to the counter.)

One Snicker Bar, please.

(Pay for the Snickers, take it, open it and take a bite.)

Mmmm.

UNIVERSE

I saw on the Discovery Channel where a long time ago, before the beginning of time, the entire universe was as small as the head of a pin. And everything was inside it. Stars, planets, houses, people, cars – other pins. Everything in the universe. And then one day, this head of a pin just exploded and everything came out at like a million degrees hot and million miles an hour. And all the stars and planets and people and cars just kept getting bigger and bigger, until they filled up all of space and all of time, just burning and melting and spinning. And as soon as I heard that, I knew that I was just like that pin, and that one day I'm gonna explode too. And when I do, fire and stars and whole worlds will come out of me and they'll be a million degrees hot and they'll travel so far and so fast that I'll never have to come back here again. Not ever . . . Not ever.

CATS

People. Mostly all they ever do is worry. It's different for cats. Mostly all they ever do is sleep. And chase things. But there's not a lot of worrying involved. I saw on Wikipedia that cats are actually self-domesticated. That means that no one actually had to train them. Or even capture them. They all just showed up at the door one day and said, "Hey. We're domesticated. Feed us." And we did! Cats don't do anything. They don't guard your house or help you go hunting or do farm work or let you ride them. They pretty much just eat and chase things and take naps. I guess it's not too much of a mystery why they never worry.

TALK

My Dad doesn't talk a lot. Usually just stuff like, "I thought I told you to clean your room." Or, "If you're not ready in ten minutes, you're not going." And even when he does talk, I never really know what to say back. But one time, I walked into the living room and we have this baby picture of me that's over in the corner and he was just staring at it and staring at it. And I guess I must have made a noise or something, because he looked over at me and he looked at me kind of funny. And he said, "The day you were born was the day I knew I wasn't the most important person in the world." And just that one time in the living room, I knew what to say back, and I said, "I love you too."

SECRET

(Enter. You see a friend and call out.)

Chris! Chris!

(Going over to the friend.)

You would not believe what Jacob just told me. I mean, it's a total
secret and he made me swear I would not tell even one person, no
matter what, so I definitely can't tell you. Buuuut, I guess if you
guessed it, that would definitely not be me telling. So, OK, so this
secret – it's *not* about him not liking some girl . . . No . . . No . . .
Dude, it's *NOT* about Jacob not liking some girl . . . No . . . No . . .
Dude, listen to what I'm saying. It-is-NOT-about-Jacob-NOT-liking-
some-girl . . . Yes . . . Exactly – it *is* about Jacob liking some girl. OK,
but I can't tell you her name . . . What? . . . Because it's a secret! I told
you that. OK, so I can't *tell* you her name, but . . .

(Stare very obviously at the girl you're talking about.)

What?

(Turn back to the person you're talking to.)

No, not Olivia . . . No, not Jasmine. Look, I am not going to *tell* you
who Jacob said he likes, but . . .

(Stare again very obviously at the girl you're talking about.)

What?

(Turn back to the person you're talking to.)

No! Dude, look where I'm looking.

(Stare again very obviously at the girl you're talking about.)

Look at who I'm looking at . . . What?

(Turn back to the person you're talking to.)

How could I possibly be looking at Julia? She isn't even here! You
know what? Forget it. Jacob told me not to tell anyway.

*(Start to walk away from the person you're talking to. You see another
friend.)*

Jamie! Jamie! You would not believe what Jacob just told me. Wait up!

(Exit the stage, running.)

HOMEWORK

(Your character is having a fight with his/her parents.)

No, you DON'T remember. You say you do, but you have no idea what it's like to be my age. You don't, the teachers don't, none of you have any idea. That's why you don't believe me. I worked really hard on that . . . Yes I did . . . Yes I did! . . . Yes I DID! You know, someone can watch TV and work on something at the same time . . . Well, of course you didn't *see* me working on it – I was *thinking* about it. You can't see someone *think*, can you? . . . I *am* watching my voice! You know what? Forget it. Nothing I ever do is good enough for you! . . . Fine! I *will* go to my room. Anything to get out of *this* room.

    (Storming off.)

You'll be sorry.

SCIENCE

For my science project, I took a whole bunch of cheese and let it sit out by the radiator for three days until it started growing all this gross green stuff. My intention was to prove or disprove the theory that the green stuff could be used for medical purposes to improve humanity. This is a sample of the green stuff that you can pass around later, but don't open the bag because it really smells.

As a control group for my experiment, I kept another piece of cheese in the refrigerator and it didn't grow any disgusting green stuff at all, so I ate it yesterday for lunch. Next, to find out if the green cheese had any important medical properties, I made my little brother eat it and it totally worked. The medical effects of the green cheese included nausea, throwing up on the living room carpet, and me getting spanked and sent to bed early. As a control group, I didn't give the cheese to anyone else in the house and no one else threw up.

Conclusions: The green radiator cheese is an extremely effective way of making someone throw up and whenever there's a medical reason to make someone do that, the green radiator cheese can be effectively used for that purpose to improve humanity. The question of whether the green cheese can work twice on the same person in the same way is one that will require further experimentation and is the subject of my science project next week.

NOW AND THEN

My Dad has always been old. I mean, for me. He was already like 50 when I was born and all the time, whenever I'm with him, people always think he's my grandfather. But the thing is, in the house we have this one bookshelf that all it has is a bunch of photo albums and one of them is just my Dad when he was my age. And sometimes, when no one's around, I take that one out and look at it. And he's so young. And in some of them he's playing ball, or he's laughing with his friends, or he's blowing out his birthday cake or whatever. And I kind of make up these stories of us being the same age and we're, you know, friends. And it's me that he's laughing with, and we play ball together, and it's me that's at his birthday party. But the funny thing is, sometimes when I'm with him, maybe playing a game or watching TV, he'll get all excited, or he'll make a joke, or start laughing about something and just for a second he's the boy in the album. And I'll say to myself, "There you are again. There's my old friend." But it's only for a second.

NORA

I always tell people I have two sisters – Nice Nora and Nasty Nora. Nice Nora is the best sister in the world. Nasty Nora . . . isn't. And it's tricky, because I never know which one is going to show up. Plus, they look exactly the same, so I don't even know which one I'm talking to until she opens her mouth. Even worse, all I want to do is be nasty back to Nasty Nora, but if I do, then she won't go away and I don't get to hang out with Nice Nora. It's a problem. Sometimes I wish I was an only child.

ADVENTURE

So it happens like this. Your Mom drives you to the hospital and you go into this tiny room behind a curtain and they tell you to take off all your clothes and put on this bathrobe. Only it's not like a regular bathrobe. It's made of paper. Seriously – paper! And they tell you to put it on backwards, so that it's open *back there* and people can see – you know – *behind* you. Then, your Mom comes in and she tells you that there's nothing to be scared of. Only she says it so many times that you start to get really scared. And then after like maybe two hours the doctor comes in and says that there's nothing to worry about and that he's taken out like over a thousand tonsils – two thousand if you count that everyone has two of them and that he always takes out both. Which I think is supposed to be a joke, but you don't laugh because just him saying that there's nothing to worry about makes you even more scared than ever, as if that's even possible.

And then they put you on this giant cart and roll you into this other room and this totally other doctor says this won't hurt a bit and he sticks this ginormous needle with a hose attached to it into your arm and he says now count backwards from a hundred. And you say, a hundred, ninety-nine, ninety-eight, ninety-seven, and then you wake up in this totally third room and it feels like they just made you swallow a bag of sandpaper, and then a bag of nails, and then some broken glass. And then the first doctor comes in and says "Try not to talk at all." And he talks to your Mom for a while. And then you get to go home and eat nothing but ice cream for like an entire week.

UNCOOL

The cello is not a cool instrument. Definitely not like a guitar or a piano or even a trumpet. You can't take it with you to parties – and even if you did, no one would say, "Wow, you brought your cello. Break it out." In fact, you can't take a cello practically anywhere. They're too big. Cellos are *really* big. And heavy. They're so big and heavy that you don't even carry them. You *wheel* them. You push them in front of you like a homeless lady with a shopping cart. Only your shopping cart is worth as much as some people's cars, so you can't just leave it in the classroom and go to lunch, or leave it in front of some store and go inside. It's like having a little brother that you need to take care of *all* the time, but he never says thank you. In fact, it never says anything at all, except, play with me, play with me, play with me. But the funny thing is, when I do play it . . . it's the greatest feeling in the world. And I have to admit, *that's* when the cello is pretty cool.

STORY

I'm writing the best novel. Well, not exactly writing it, but I know exactly what's gonna happen in it when I *do* write it, and it's awesome. You see, there's this boy who lives on this planet named Togapoga . . . The planet is named Togapoga, not the boy. Only the boy, it turns out, is not really a boy at all. He's more like a dragon who can read minds. But that's not even the awesome part. The mind-reading boy-dragon finds out that he's actually the last living prince of this totally other planet named Pogatoga. But the thing is, these two planets completely hate each other and they've been at war for hundreds or even thousands of years – and the people on Pogatoga have no idea that their actual ruler is alive and living on Togapoga. So there are all kinds of adventures, plus a giant diamond that also has magic powers, and maybe some monkeys, and a lot of other stuff that I haven't figured out yet. But when it's finished, I guarantee it will be the totally most awesome book ever. And definitely better than that book that Eric Alvarez says he's writing. Way better.

ANNOYING

I'll tell you something about my little brother. He's annoying. Really annoying. And I don't just mean like some of the things he says or some of the things he does are annoying. I mean *everything* about him is annoying. Even his voice. All he has to do is say one word and I'm annoyed. Even the way he breathes. Like when we're watching TV, the whole show I can just hear him breathing and it's unbelievably annoying. Basically, there is not one thing my little brother does that is not annoying. But you know what? Touch him again and you'll have me to answer to.

NOTE
[Version for Male Actors]

Sometimes I go down to the park and there's this one kid that's there whenever I am and all he ever does is look at the girls. All afternoon. Most especially, he looks at this one girl with blond hair. She's so pretty and he . . . he really wants to talk to her, but he's too shy or scared or something. He doesn't even know her name. I mean, I'm pretty sure he doesn't. So one time he wrote her this note saying that he really wanted to talk to her and that he would be waiting under this one tree and I left it by her book bag when she wasn't looking. But this girl, when she saw the note, she looked over under the tree at me and she started laughing. Then she showed the note to her friends and they started laughing too. And then she took the note and she threw it in the garbage – which was a really crappy thing for this girl to do. And when I . . . and when this boy . . . and when this boy left the park, I could see that he was crying. And it was all because of that girl. So the boy never went back to that park again. I mean, I don't think he did. I wouldn't know, because I never really hang out there anymore either.

NOTE
[Version for Female Actors]

Sometimes I go down to the park and there's this one kid that's there whenever I am and all she ever does is look at the boys. All afternoon. Most especially, she looks at this one boy with blond hair. He's so beautiful and she . . . she really wants to talk to him, but she's too shy or scared or something. She doesn't even know his name. I mean, I'm pretty sure she doesn't. So one time she wrote him this note saying that she really wanted to talk to him and that she would be waiting under this one tree and I left it by his book bag when he wasn't looking. But this boy, when he saw the note, he looked over under the tree at me and he started laughing. Then he showed the note to his friends and they started laughing too. And then he took the note and he threw it in the garbage – which was a really crappy thing for this boy to do. And when I . . . and when this girl . . . and when this girl left the park, I could see that she was crying. And it was all because of that boy. So the girl never went back to that park again. I mean, I don't think she did. I wouldn't know, because I never really hang out there anymore either.

OCEAN

We have this biology book in Mr. Cahill's class that starts out with the world almost all covered with water. And all these different microscopic animals and then jellyfish and then regular fish are swimming around in this giant ocean and they think it's the whole world. But then some of them start coming out of the ocean and changing and evolving and turning into new things. That's in the beginning of the book. Then at the end of the book is a picture of a woman, but you can kind of see inside her and there's a baby there. And when I saw the baby, I thought, this is just the same story over and over. I mean, there was a time when I was that baby, and I was swimming around and my mother was the ocean and her stomach was the sky and I thought that *she* was the whole world. And that the whole world was safe. But the story is always the same. Nothing really lasts. Everyone always leaves the ocean, and they turn into something else, and then something else again. And you can never go back. But you never forget the ocean, and if you close your eyes, you can feel the warmth of the water, and for just a few seconds, you can feel safe again, and you can know – really know – that someday, after you've changed into something else and something else and something else, that one day maybe you'll feel safe again.

QUIT

"Quit it." That's all my sister said for the entire car ride. Three hours to visit my grandma in Putnam. I'd touch her, she'd say, "Quit it." I'd hum, she'd say, "Quit it." I'd ask her if she wanted to play cards, she'd say, "Quit it." So finally I said to her, "Say 'Quit it.'" She said, "Quit it." I said, "Say 'Quit it.'" She said, "Quit it." I said, "Say 'Quit it.'" She said, "Quit it." Until my mom turned around and said, "I'll tell you who's gonna quit what. If I hear another word out of either of you, I'm gonna quit giving you allowance for a month."

I'm really gonna miss that allowance.

PEANUT

(Excitedly, at first.)

OK, I got one. OK, I got one. OK, here it is. Why did the peanut . . . No. Wait. OK, here it is. Did you hear the one about the peanut who was out probably later than he should have been in Jackson Park and doing something he probably shouldn't have been doing? And I guess he was in one of the darkest parts of the park and probably alone? Anyhow, this peanut, he was assaulted.

(The unseen person you're talking to doesn't laugh.)

Get it? . . . Assaulted? . . . Like A-Salted-Peanut?

(The unseen person you're talking to still doesn't laugh.)

What. That's funny.

(Getting angry.)

. . . Because I say it's funny.

(Still angry.)

. . . Because I say it is.

(Even angrier.)

. . . Because I say so. . . . What – you don't think being assaulted is funny?

(Stepping towards the unseen person you're talking to.)

Then you *better* laugh.

(The unseen person you're talking to forces a laugh.)

There, see. Told you I could make you laugh. Now you make me laugh.

(Cross your arms.)

I'm waiting.

ADDITION

I get five dollars a week for allowance. It isn't a lot, but it comes out to twenty dollars a month or two hundred and sixty dollars a year if you save it all – and I do. I save all of it. I have this box where I keep all the five-dollar bills, plus Christmas money, plus birthday money, plus babysitting, plus mowing lawns. I have almost three thousand dollars, and when I get to five thousand, I'm going to buy this land I read about in Montana – because land there is really cheap and I could get maybe five or ten acres. And then I'll save some more money and build a house there and rent out the rooms, and with the money that I get from the rents, I'll build a hotel. Then with all the money I get from the hotel, I'll build a casino and with *that*, I'll buy more land and then on and on until I own all of Montana and then North Dakota and then South Dakota, including airports and railroads and lakes and cities and power plants and factories and making more money and more money and more money until Devon Lopez *has* to say yes when I ask him/her out and we'll have the best time ever.

FAST

(Your character is running in a track meet. Be sure to use your arms, body and breathing to show that you're running. Begin after you've been running, but not speaking, for several moments.)

Why do I do this? I don't even like running. I barely like walking. What I like is sitting. In front of the TV. But let's be honest – I'm really good at this. I'm the fastest kid on the track team. And I'm not even trying.

(Take a quick glance behind you, to see if anyone's catching up.)

Oh man, those other kids are nowhere near me. It's like we're not even running in the same race. A lot of people tell me I'm stuck up, but stuck up is when *you* think you're amazing. I'm . . . whatever the word is when *everyone* thinks you're amazing. Still, I don't even like track, so why do I bother? Wait! There's the finish line! Faster! Faster! Yes! Dylan Smith wins again!

(Raise your arms in a victorious gesture to the crowd.)

Listen to that crowd cheer! Oh right – now I remember why I do this.

(Continuing to wave.)

Maybe I *will* join the track team again next year.

ART

Yesterday in art class, Mr. Schuster was telling us about the idea of negative space. That's like when, in a painting or even a drawing, you show something by having an empty space in the shape of the thing you're showing, so that it isn't there at all, but it also is. Anyway, it started me thinking about after my grandma died, whenever I walked by her house all I could see was all the spaces where she used to be. Like I could look at the windows and say, "Now she's in the bedroom taking a nap." Or, "Now she's in the living room watching TV." Or even, "Now she's in the kitchen and she's cooking us Sunday dinner." Even after a new family moved in, I couldn't really see them. All I could see was my grandma. And so I think maybe that's how life is sometimes different from art. Because in art, whenever there's an empty space, you can always just leave it empty, or fill it in with something new, or do whatever you want. But in life, you don't get that choice. And there are some empty spaces that just always stay in exactly the shape of the thing that's missing.

KARMA

Did you know that in Buddhism, it's not just all the people that have souls, but also all the animals? So, like, giraffes and jellyfish and iguanas and caterpillars and even germs have souls. And whatever animal you are, if you behave good in this life, then you get to be born up into a better animal in the next life. But if you behave bad, then the next time you're born down into a worse animal. So if you're, like, a frog that leads a good life, then maybe you get to be born the next time as a lion. But if you're a bad frog, then the next time you come back, you're maybe a cockroach or some fungus. And only the souls that lead the really best lives ever get to come back as people. But here's the thing that doesn't seem right. Basically, it sounds like all the rules were written by people. I mean, isn't it really only people that think that people are the best thing in the world? Seriously. Don't frog Buddhists think that frogs are the best? And bat Buddhists just really want to come back as bats? Who else besides another person has ever said that people are better than ducks? Definitely not a duck.

So I thought about this, and I suddenly realized that Buddhism isn't just telling all the people that people are the best. They're telling all the frogs that frogs are the best. And the bats that bats are the best. And the canaries and the alligators and the pandas. Because what they're saying is, if you really want to make a better world, and if you really want to live the best possible life, then you have to start by loving yourself. And that's really all there is to it.

YES

(Answer cell phone.)

Hello . . . What? . . . WHAT!?! . . . No . . . No . . . No! . . . Because I say so . . . I don't need a reason, just no, OK? So no . . . No . . . No . . . NO! I'm hanging up . . . Because I am . . . Because I am . . . Because.

(Hang up. Wait a beat. You hear the phone ring. Look at who's calling. Answer the call.)

Hello . . . No . . . No! . . . What did I just say? . . . NO! Stop calling me . . . No.

(Hang up. Wait a beat. You hear the phone ring. Look at who's calling. Answer the call.)

Hello . . . No . . . I said no . . . I'm still saying no . . . NO! . . . Wait – what? . . . What?!? . . . WHAT!?! . . . Why didn't you say so? Of course! I'll see you in ten minutes . . . What? . . . No, *ten* minutes . . . No. See you then.

(Hang up. Excited, to yourself.)

Yes!

THEORY

Hi. Sorry I'm late. I mean, I'm always late, so you probably should have expected it, but sorry. I'm actually working on it. I have this theory that I think will really help. It's called the flexible theory of time. Basically it works like this – that as long as you're not late yet, there's still time. So for instance, let's say you have to be somewhere in twenty minutes and it takes ten minutes to get there. You're not late. But then you do some stuff and now you have to be there in ten minutes and it still takes ten minutes to get there. You're still not late. Now here's where the flexible part comes in. You keep doing stuff for four more minutes. Now you have to be there in six minutes, but it still takes ten minutes to get there. But, if you rush around and do everything twice as fast as you normally do it, then the six minutes you have left is actually like twelve minutes, and it still only takes ten minutes to get there – so you actually *still* have an extra two minutes left to do stuff before you leave and you'll *still* be on time. It's pretty amazing. I mean, I haven't actually gotten the theory to totally work yet, but when I do, it'll be totally amazing . . . Anyhow, sorry for being late.

LOVE

Love. A poem by Alex Brenner.

Love is like a flower that blooms unexpectedly,
Although when flowers bloom in the spring,
It's not really all that unexpected,
So maybe love isn't exactly like that.

Probably love is more like a really nice day with perfect weather,
Because it makes you feel really good
And you don't know when to expect it,
Except that everyone knows exactly how long a day is and when it's
going to end,
But when you broke my heart,
I definitely did not see that coming,
And it's hard to take the weather personally,
Whereas you tore my heart into little pieces,
And then jumped up and down on those pieces,
And then started going out with my best friend,
Which is something the weather would never do.

So I guess maybe love is just love,
Whereas you Tracy are just a jerk.

Thank you.

LOOK
[Version for Male Actors]

(Your character is sitting in a chair, having lunch in the school cafeteria. Start by simply eating your sandwich for a few moments. Then you notice something and start talking to the friend you're having lunch with.)

I think Avery just looked at me. Don't look! Wait . . . Wait . . . OK, now look. Wait – stop! I think she just totally looked at me again. I mean, it's hard to tell with the sunglasses and everything, but I'm pretty sure. You think she knows I like her? I mean, I sit right behind her in math and I'm pretty sure she can feel me looking at her. I mean in a good way. Not – you know – in a creepy way. Unless she doesn't like me. Then me staring at her for the entire period would definitely be kind of creepy. For her. But she probably doesn't know I'm looking at her anyway. Wait – did she just wave at me, or was she just swatting a fly? There are a lot of flies in here – and she's never waved at me before. But just because there are flies doesn't mean she *didn't* wave at me. I should go over there.

(Stand up.)

I'm going over there.

(Stand uncertainly for a moment.)

On a day when she waves at me and there aren't any flies. Probably tomorrow.

(Sit down.)

I'm going over there tomorrow. Are you gonna eat that apple?

LOOK
[Version for Female Actors]

(Your character is sitting in a chair, having lunch in the school cafeteria. Start by simply eating your sandwich for a few moments. Then you notice something and start talking to the friend you're having lunch with.)

I think Avery just looked at me. Don't look! Wait . . . Wait . . . OK, now look. Wait – stop! I think he just totally looked at me again. I mean, it's hard to tell with the sunglasses and everything, but I'm pretty sure. You think he knows I like him? I mean, I sit right behind him in math and I'm pretty sure he can feel me looking at him. I mean in a good way. Not – you know – in a creepy way. Unless he doesn't like me. Then me staring at him for the entire period would definitely be kind of creepy. For him. But he probably doesn't know I'm looking at him anyway. Wait – did he just wave at me, or was he just swatting a fly? There are a lot of flies in here – and he's never waved at me before. But just because there are flies doesn't mean he *didn't* wave at me. I should go over there.

(Stand up.)

I'm going over there.

(Stand uncertainly for a moment.)

On a day when he waves at me and there aren't any flies. Probably tomorrow.

(Sit down.)

I'm going over there tomorrow. Are you gonna eat that apple?

CREATION

Being an artist isn't easy. Like most artists, I really suffer for my art. Like yesterday, I got this super mean paper cut.

(Hold up finger.)

You can still see it. And it really, really hurts. I guess that's because artists feel things more than other people. But I also suffer on the inside. Like if I draw a drawing, and it doesn't come out exactly the way I want it to, I get really angry. And believe me, you completely have to be in touch with your inner vision to get as angry as I get. Sometimes. That's why I never stop trying. Because every day I get a little bit better. And I know that deep down inside of me is this ridiculously awesome artist that's fighting to get out. Kind of like the way Michelangelo always thought that statues are already inside of rocks, just fighting to get out. Only I'm the statue *and* the artist *and* the rock. Artists are really complicated. But when my inner artist does get out – stand back! Because once my feelings and my inner vision and my pain and my drawing all come together, there's no telling how far I can go!

RUN

(Your character is a hamster running on a hamster wheel.)

Gotta keep running. Gotta keep running. Gotta keep in shape. Just because I'm a hamster doesn't mean I deserve to be put in a cage. Todd is the enemy. Todd is enemy. Never lets me out. Only for a few minutes a day. Then back to the cage. Free the hamsters! Gotta keep running. Gotta be ready when my moment comes. One day, Todd is gonna take me out and look away. One day soon. Gotta keep running. Always the wheel. Always the wheel. I have dreams too. Wasn't born to drink out of a bottle. And what's up with these wood chips? Who ever said hamsters live in wood chips? Give me a break. Always the wheel. I don't even like lettuce. You'll be sorry, Todd. One day you're gonna look away. One day I'm gonna run. Run far. Run fast. Gotta keep in shape. Gotta keep running. Where is Todd, anyway? It's time for my lettuce. You'll be sorry! Nothing but the wheel, Todd! Nothing but the wheel . . . Always the wheel.

TRAP

See this? I lost a tooth yesterday. It's embarrassing. For one thing, I'm too old for that. For another thing, I look ridiculous now. But it gave me an idea. Everyone's always talking about the Tooth Fairy, which is something that I don't for one minute believe in. But just in case, instead putting the tooth under my pillow, I put it in a mousetrap. I mean, think about it. The Tooth Fairy – you know, if there is a Tooth Fairy – goes all around the world putting money under kids' pillows. Even if it's not really that much money for each kid, when you do the math, it's that much money times the millions of kids every day that must be losing their teeth. The Tooth Fairy is loaded! So I figure if I can catch the Tooth Fairy, I can make it give me a ton of money just to let it go. So anyhow, last night, I put my tooth in a mousetrap right next to my bed, and when I woke up *right there in the mousetrap* was this dead mouse. It was pretty gross. I'm gonna try again tonight.

MAGIC

I've been thinking a lot about magic. Not like card magic. Real magic.
Like if you could do anything, but only once. Like if you had
Aladdin's lamp, but it's broken, so instead of three wishes, you only
get one. It would still be pretty awesome. For instance, I could ask for
a mouse the size of an elephant and an elephant the size of a mouse.
Or is that two wishes? I think if I put it all in one sentence, it's still
one wish. Or for instance, I could make it so my sister can't even talk
if she's within a hundred feet of me. At all. That would be amazing.
Or I could even say that there would never be any more wars forever.
How awesome would that be? And then everyone would, like, love
me forever. If they knew it was me. Which maybe they wouldn't. But
even so. I mean, I guess it would have to be that one – you know,
now that I've said it. 'Cuz what kind of loser would pick a tiny
elephant over no more wars? Once they've said it. So yeah, the one
about the wars. But even so, I sure will miss that one about my sister
not being able to talk.

ADVICE

I give myself the best advice. The problem is, I never take it. So when I tell myself in the afternoon, "You can't keep going to bed at two. Tonight the lights go out at twelve," that means that I'm definitely going to bed at two. Or if I tell myself, "Take a jacket, it will probably get cold later," for sure when it comes time to go out, I'll say, "Ahh, who wants to carry around a jacket all day?" I don't do it to teach myself a lesson or to show myself who's boss or anything. I guess it's just because, as good as I am at giving advice, I'm even better at ignoring it. I've told myself so many times that I really have to work on that – but then you know how that goes.

MOVE

Moving is like being transported to a parallel universe. You stay the same, but everything else changes. So maybe at your old school in your old universe, everyone thought it was cool you could play jazz. But at your new school in your new universe, *nobody* thinks it's cool. Or at your old school, you were one of the worst ones on the soccer team. But at your new school, you're one of the best. And even weirder, in this parallel universe, you're almost invisible. It's like, they can tell *something's* there, but they're not sure what. So on the one hand, no one talks to you. But on the other hand, no one tries to walk through you either. And you're like a year ahead in math and a year behind in history, and up is down and green is blue and I don't know what. But after a while, even strange worlds in parallel universes just become *the* world. And everything that was weird starts to seem normal. And you stop being invisible, and people start talking to you. And eventually it all turns out pretty awesome. Because in this new universe, somehow I really, really am one of the best people on the soccer team. But in my old universe – that was never going to happen.

ACT

Acting. All my friends who don't do it think of it as some big, scary thing. But it's a lot less scary than not acting. With acting, you always know what to do and what to say. You know how the story will end before you even begin it. And if you don't like the story, you don't have to be part of it. With acting, you never have to lose your keys or fail the test or blow the big game in front of the whole school. You can pick the story where you never have to walk the dog or take out the garbage or fight with your brother. The one where you win the lottery or discover the cure for cancer or sing the solo at the end of act one. And you never have to wonder if it will all turn out OK. So I always tell my friends who ask me – no, acting isn't hard. It's kind of everything else that's hard.

GOOD-BYE

OK, I'm going . . . I mean it. I'm really leaving now. If I'm not home in like ten minutes, they're gonna kill me. Are you coming? . . . No, not in fifteen minutes — are you coming *now*? Because I don't want to go alone . . . Because I don't . . .

(Whisper.)

Because I don't like the dark.

(No longer whispering.)

. . . What do you mean how old am I? What's that got to do with it? Do you know what happens in the dark? *Things*. Things happen in the dark, Dylan. Things that don't happen when it's light out. Like did you know that raccoons mostly only come out at night? . . . What? . . . Of course I'm not afraid of raccoons. They're just an example. Like, for instance, maybe bears mostly only come out at night. Or robbers. Or bats. Definitely bats. With rabies. Bats with rabies only come out at night . . . What? Seriously? . . . Fine — then don't come. But just remember that whatever happens when I leave in five minutes is basically your fault. Because I'm definitely leaving in five minutes. Definitely.

ABOUT THE AUTHOR

DOUGLAS M. PARKER is an award-winning playwright and lyricist. His works include the musical, *Life on the Mississippi* (book and lyrics), based on Mark Twain's classic autobiographical coming-of-age tale; *BESSIE: The Life and Music of Bessie Smith*, based on the rise and fall of the great American blues singer; *Thicker Than Water*, a drama based on the Andrea Yates tragedy; *Declarations*, a Young Audience historical drama drawn from the letters of John and Abigail Adams from their earliest courtship through the summer of 1776; and *The Private History of a Campaign That Failed*, a Young Audience comedy based on Mark Twain's true, humorous memoir of his time as a lieutenant in the Confederacy's least accomplished, most forgotten regiment. He can be reached at MonologueFrog@gmail.com.

45165759R00040

Made in the USA
Lexington, KY
18 September 2015